Deep Learning

A Comprehensive Guide for Beginners

Contents

Chapter 1: Machine Learning Basics

1.1 Introduction

Deep learning could be a special kind of machine learning. So as to grasp deep learning in best approach, one must have a strong thoughtful of the required rules of machine learning. This chapter delivers an ephemeral course in the foremost important general rules that will be applied throughout the remainder of the book.

Machine Learning, because the name recommends, delivers machines with the aptitude to learn unconventionally based mostly on experiences, observations and analyzing forms at intervals a given data set deprived of overtly programming. When we have a tendency to write a program or a code for a few explicit aims, we are literally writing a sure set of commands that the machine will follow. While in machine learning, we tend to input a data set through which the machine can learn by classifying and analyzing the patterns in the information set and learn to gross decisions separately primarily based on its observations and learning from the dataset.

Machine learning is an application of artificial intelligence (AI) that describes systems the capability to inevitably learn and endure experience without being overtly programmed. Machine learning emphases on the expansion of computer programs which will entree information and use it learn for themselves.

The procedure of learning starts with observations or data, like examples, direct expertise, or instruction, so as to look for patterns in data and create better choices in the longer term engineered on the examples that we deliver. The primary aim is to allow the computers learn automatically while not human intervention or assist and regulate activities accordingly.

1.2 Why we require Machine Learning

Data is increasing daily, and it's unbelievable to spot all of the data with higher speed and higher correctness. More than 80p.c of the info is amorphous that's audio, videos, photos, documents, graphs, etc. Discovery patterns in information on planet earth is impossible for human intelligences. The data has been very huge, the time taken to calculate would surge, and this is often where Machine Learning comes into act, to help folks with important data in minimum time.

1.3 The difference between Machine Learning, Artificial Intelligence and Deep Learning

While learning concerning machine learning fundamentals, one typically complicates Machine Learning, Artificial Intelligence and Deep Learning.

We familiar with the term "Artificial Intelligence." After all, it's been a well-liked attention in movies like The Terminator, The Matrix, and Ex Machina (a private favorite of mine). But you will have recently been hearing regarding other terms like "Machine Learning" and "Deep Learning," sometimes used interchangeably with artificial intelligence. As a significance, the alteration between artificial intelligence, machine learning, and deep learning can be terribly unclear.

Let's dig deeper therefore that you'll be able to recognize which is best for your precise use case: artificial intelligence, machine learning, or deep learning.

What is artificial intelligence?

As the name suggests, artificial intelligence can be roughly understood to mean integrating human intelligence to machines.

9

Artificial intelligence is the broad concept that consists of everything from Good Antiquated AI (GOFAI) all the means to futuristic technologies like deep learning.

Whenever a machine finishes tasks primarily based on a set of postulated rules that solve problems (algorithms), such an "intelligent" behavior is what is referred to as artificial intelligence.

For example, such machines will transfer and manipulate objects, establish whether someone has elevated the hands, or resolve different issues.

AI-powered machines are sometimes categorized into 2 groups: general and slender. The general artificial intelligence AI machines will logically solve issues, like those mentioned above.

The narrow intelligence AI machines can achieve special tasks terribly well, often better than humans-though they are limited in scope.

The technology used for categorizing pictures on Pinterest could be a sample of slim AI.

What is machine learning?

As the name suggests, machine learning can be loosely understood to mean sanctioning pc systems with the aptitude to "learn".

The meaning of ML is to empower machines to learn by themselves using the delivered knowledge and create precise predictions.

ML could be a subset of artificial intelligence; in fact, it's simply a way for realizing AI.

It could be a process of training algorithms such that they will learn the way to make choices.

Coaching in machine learning includes giving a ton of data to the algorithm and allowing it to find out a lot of about the organized info.

What is deep learning?

As earlier mentioned, deep learning may be a subset of ML; of course, it's merely a process for recognizing machine learning. In other words, DL is the subsequent development of machine learning.

DL algorithms are roughly enthused by the knowledge processing patterns found within the human brain.

Just like we tend to use our brains to identify patterns and categorize many types of knowledge, deep learning algorithms will be trained to accomplish the same errands for machines.

The brain typically tries to decode the knowledge it obtains. It attains this through labelling and assigning the things into varied classes.

Whenever we accept a replacement data, the brain tries to check it to a known item before making sense of it- which is the same concept deep learning algorithms use.

For example, artificial neural networks (ANNs) are a reasonably algorithm that aim to emulate the way our brains build decisions.

Comparing deep learning vs machine learning will support you to acknowledge their elusive differences.

Putting it together in an exceedingly broader context:

- Artificial intelligence is the capability of a machine or computer system to emulate intelligent human behavior.

- Machine learning is an application of AI concerned with receiving computer systems to progress their accuracy at tasks using data alone, without precise programming.

- Deep learning is a subfield of machine learning involved with modeling high-level data concepts to determine high-level meaning from unstructured data.

- Neural networks are systems designed to imitator the human brain and increasingly improve at errands using algorithms and labeled data.

1.2 Machine Learning Algorithm

We tend to begin with an explanation of what a learning algorithm is, and present an example: the linear regression algorithm. We have a tendency to then proceed to explain how the take a look at of acceptable the coaching data differs from the challenge of discovery patterns that simplify to new data. Most machine learning algorithms have settings referred to as hyperparameters that has got

13

to be determined external to the educational algorithm itself; we tend to discuss how to set these using further knowledge.

Most machine learning algorithms will be classified into the classes of supervised learning and unsupervised learning; we describe these categories and offer some samples of easy learning algorithms from every group.

1.4.1 Kinds of Machine Learning

Machine Learning primarily divided into three categories, which are as follows

- Supervised
- Unsupervised
- Reinforcement

- **Supervised Learning:**

  Supervised Learning is the first type of machine learning, in which labelled knowledge used to coach the algorithms. In supervised learning, algorithms are trained using marked information, where the input and also the output are known. We input the data in the learning algorithm as a group of inputs, that is

14

termed as Features, denoted by X together with the matching outputs, which is designated by Y, and the algorithm learns by associating its actual production with correct outputs to get errors.

It then modifies the model consequently. The raw knowledge separated into 2 components. The first part is for training the algorithm, and the opposite section used for take a look at the trained algorithm.

- **Unsupervised Learning:**

The Supervised Learning primarily divided into two parts which are as follows:

- **Regression:**

Regression is the sort of Supervised Learning in which labelled knowledge used, and this knowledge is employed to create guesses in a continuous type. The output of the input is usually ongoing, and also the graph is linear. Regression could be a form of analytical modelling process which examines the connection between a reliant on variable [Outputs] and freelance variable [Inputs]. This technique used for predicting the weather, time series modelling, method optimization. Ex: - One of the examples of the regression technique is House Price Prediction, where the worth of the house can predict from the inputs like No of rooms, Locality, Ease of transport, Age of house, Area of a home.

There are several Regression algorithms are existing in machine learning, which will use for dislike regression applications. Some of the key regression algorithms are as follows-

➢ **Simple Linear Regression:**

In easy linear regression, we forecast scores on one variable from the ratings on a second variable. The variable we are forecasting is named the criterion variable and called Y. The variable we tend to are basing our predictions on is termed the

16

predictor variable and denoted to as

> **Multiple Linear Regression:**

Multiple linear regression is one amongst the algorithms of regression technique, and it is the most common type of linear regression analysis. As a predictive analysis, the multiple linear regression is employed to elucidate the link between one dependent variable with 2 or more than two independent variables. The freelance variables will be continuous or categorical.

> **Polynomial Regression:**

Polynomial regression is another form of regression in which the maximum power of the independent variable is more than 1. In this regression technique, the best fit line is not a straight line instead it is in the form of a curve.

Polynomial regression is another kind of regression in that the maximum power of the independent variable is additional than one. In this regression technique, the simplest work line isn't a straight line instead it is in the form of a curve.

➤ **Support Vector Regression:**

Support Vector Regression will be applied not only to regression difficulties, but it also utilized in the case of classification. It covers all the options that describe most margin algorithm. Linear learning machine charting leans a non-linear operate into high dimensional kernel-induced feature space. The system volume was measured by parameters that do not depend on the dimensionality of feature area.

➤ **Lasso Regression:**

Lasso regression is a kind of linear

regression that uses reduction. Reduction is where knowledge values shrunk towards a central purpose, just like the mean. The lasso method inspires simple, sparse models (i.e. models with fewer parameters). This actual quite regression is compatible for models showing high levels of multicollinearity or when you wish to automate convinced components of model selection, like variable selection/parameter elimination.

• **Classification:**

Classification is the kind of Supervised Learning in which labelled knowledge will use, and this information is employed to make guesses during a non-continuous type. The output of the knowledge isn't continuous, and also the graph is nonlinear. In the classification technique, the algorithm learns from the data input given to it and then uses this learning to classify new observation.

There are many Classification algorithms are present in machine learning, that used for dislike classification applications. Some of the first classification algorithms are as follows-

➢ **Naïve Bayes:**

It is also a classification technique. The logic behind this classification technique is to use Bayes theorem for making classifiers. The supposition is that the forecasters are independent. In simple words, it assumes that the presence of a particular feature in a class is unrelated to the presence of any other feature. Below is

20

the equation for Bayes theorem

$$P\left(\frac{A}{B}\right)=\frac{P\left(\frac{B}{A}\right)P(A)}{P(B)}$$

The Naïve Bayes model is easy to make and particularly useful for large data sets.

➤ **Choice Tree:**

Choice tree may be a supervised learning algorithm that's largely used for classification issues. Basically, it's a classifier expressed as recursive divider based on the independent variables. Selection tree has nodes that kind the rooted tree. Rooted tree could be a directed tree with a node called "root". Root does not have any incoming edges and all the opposite nodes have one

21

incoming edge. These nodes are known as leaves or alternative nodes. For example, consider the following selection tree to work out whether or not a person is fit or not.

➢ **Random Forest:**

It is a supervised classification algorithm. The advantage of random forest algorithm is that it can be used for each classification and regression reasonably issues. Basically, it's the group of alternative trees (i.e., forest) or you can say ensemble of the choice trees. The basic concept of random forest is that each tree offers a classification and also the forest chooses the best classifications from them. Followings are the advantages of Random Forest algorithm -

Random forest classifier can be used for both classification and regression tasks.

- They can grip the missing values.
- It won't over fit the model even if we have a greater number of trees in the forest.

➢ **K Nearest Neighbor:**

It is employed for both classification and regression of the difficulties. It is broadly used to solve classification problems. The primary concept of this algorithm is that it used to stock all the accessible cases and classifies new cases by majority votes of its k neighbors. The case being then allotted to the category that is the most common between its K-nearest neighbors, measured by a distance function. The distance perform will be Euclidean, Minkowski and Hamming distance.

➢ **Support Vector Machine:**

It is used for both classification and regression problems. But mostly it is used for classification problems. The key concept of SVM is to plot every data item as a point in n-dimensional space with the value of every feature being the value of a particular organize. Here n would be the features we would have.

1.4 Machine Learning in Practice

Machine learning algorithms are only a very minor part of by means of machine learning in practice as a data analyst or data scientist. In training, the process often looks like:

- Start Loop
- ✓ Recognize the primary, prior knowledge and goals. Talk to primary experts. Often the goals are very unclear. You often have more things to try then you can possibly implement.
- ✓ Data integration, selection, cleaning and pre-processing. This is often the most time-consuming part. It is important to have high quality data. The more data you have, the more it sucks because the data is dirty. Garbage in, garbage out.
- ✓ Learning models. The fun part. This part is very developed. The tools are general.
- ✓ Interpreting results. Sometimes it does not matter how the model works as long it delivers results. Another primary require that the model is comprehensible. You will be dared by human experts.

✓ Consolidating and organizing discovered knowledge. The majority of projects that are effective in the lab are not used in practice. It is very firm to get something used.

- End Loop

It is not a one-shot procedure, it is a series. You require to run the loop until you get a result that you can use in practice. Also, the data can alter, demanding a new loop.

Now we will more confer topics of Applied Mathematics for Machine Learning.

Let's get started!

Chapter 2: Applied Mathematics for Deep Learning

2.1 Introduction

This part of the book presents the elementary mathematical perceptions required to comprehend deep learning. We start with general ideas from applied math that allow us to define functions of many variables, find the highest and lowest points on these functions and count degrees of belief.

Mathematics plays an important role as it makes the foundation for programming for these two streams. And in this course, we've covered exactly that. We planned a finish syllabus to assist you master the mathematical basis required for writing programs and algorithms for Artificial Intelligence and Machine Learning.

The book covers three key mathematical theories: Linear Algebra, Multivariate Calculus and Probability Theory.

2.1.1 Maths for Deep Learning?

There are many reasons why the mathematics of Deep Learning is significant and I will describe some of them below:

28

- Choosing the correct algorithm which contains considering accuracy, number of parameters and number of features, training time and model difficulty.
- Classifying underfitting and overfitting by recognizing the Bias-Variance tradeoff.
- Approximating the right confidence interval and doubt.
- Selecting parameter settings and authentication strategies.

2.1.2 What Level of Maths Do You Require?

The primary question when tiresome to grasp an interdisciplinary arena like Deep Learning is the number of maths necessary and the level of maths required to recognize these techniques. The answer to the present question is multidimensional and depends on the amount and a focus of the individual. Research in mathematical preparations and theoretical progression of Deep Learning is ongoing and some researchers are working on additional advance techniques. I can describe what I believe to be the smallest amount level of arithmetic required to be a Deep Learning Scientist/Engineer and the importance of every mathematical concept.

- **Linear Algebra:** In ML, Linear Algebra comes up universally. Topics like Principal Component Analysis (PCA), Singular Value Decomposition (SVD), Eigen decomposition of a matrix, LU Decomposition, QR Decomposition/Factorization, Symmetric Matrices, Orthogonalization & Orthonormalization, Matrix Operations, Projections, Eigenvalues & Eigenvectors, Vector Spaces and Norms are needed for considerate the optimization method used for deep learning. The wonderful issue regarding Linear Algebra is that there are so many online resources.

- **Probability Theory and Statistics:** Machine Learning and Statistics are not very dislike arenas. Actually, someone recently defined Machine Learning as 'doing statistics on a Mac'. Some of the necessary Statistical and Probability Theory needed for ML are Probability Rules & Axioms, Bayes' Theorem, Random Variables, Variance and Expectation, Conditional and Joint Distributions,

Standard Distributions (Bernoulli, Binomial, Multinomial, Uniform and Gaussian), Moment Generating Functions, Maximum Likelihood Estimation (MLE), Prior and Posterior, Maximum a Posteriori Estimation (MAP) and Sampling Process.

- **Multivariate Calculus:** Some of the essential topics contain Dislikeable and Integral Calculus, Partial Derivatives, Vector-Values Functions, Directional Gradient, Hessian, Jacobian, Laplacian and Lagragian Distribution.

- **Algorithms and Difficult Optimizations:** This is important for recognizing the computational efficiency and scalability of our Machine Learning Algorithm and for exploiting sparsity in our datasets. Information of data structures (Binary Trees, Hashing, Heap, Stack etc.), Dynamic Programming, Randomized & Sublinear Algorithm, Graphs, Gradient/Stochastic Descents and Primal-Dual process are required.

- **Others:** This contains of other Math subjects not covered in the four primary areas described above. They contain Real and Difficult Analysis (Sets and Sequences, Topology, Metric Spaces,

Single-Valued and Continuous Functions, Limits, Cauchy Kernel, Fourier Transforms), Information Theory (Entropy, Information Gain), Function Spaces and Manifolds.

2.2 Linear Algebra

In this section we have a tendency to gift important classes of spaces in which our knowledge can live and our processes can take place: vector spaces, normed spaces, metric areas, inner product areas and outer product spaces. Usually describing, these are distinct in such a method on imprisonment a number of important properties of Euclidean area however in a very more over-all method.

Linear Algebra may be an unending procedure of mathematics and is applied through science and engineering as a result of it allows you to prototypical natural marvels and to compute them proficiently. As a result of it is a type of unceasing and not discrete arithmetic, a lot of pc specialists do not have a lot of experience with it. Linear Algebra is additionally central to nearly all parts of arithmetic like geometry and purposeful analysis.

So, if you really need to be a knowledgeable in this arena, you'll should master the components of Linear Algebra that are important for Machine Learning. In Linear Algebra, data is signified by linear equations, that are presented in the shape of matrices and vectors.

2.2.1 Notation

Notation	Meaning
$\mathbb{R}$	set of real numbers
$\mathbb{R}_n$	set (vector space) of n-tuples of real numbers, endowed with the usual inner product
$\mathbb{R}_{m \times n}$	set (vector space) of m-by-n matrices
δ_{ij}	Kronecker delta, i.e. $\delta_{ij} = 1$ if $i = j$, 0 otherwise
$\nabla f(\mathbf{x})$	gradient of the function f at $\mathbf{x}$
$\nabla^2 f(\mathbf{x})$	Hessian of the function f at $\mathbf{x}$
$\mathbf{A}_>$	transpose of the matrix $\mathbf{A}$
Ω	sample space
$P(A)$	probability of event A
$p(X)$	distribution of random variable X
$p(x)$	probability density/mass function evaluated at x
A_c	complement of event A
$A \cup\!\!\!\cdot\; B$	union of A and B, with the extra requirement that $A \cap B = \emptyset$
$E[X]$	expected value of random variable X
$Var(X)$	variance of random variable X
$Cov(X, Y)$	covariance of random variables X and Y

2.2.2 Vector Space

Vector spaces are the elementary setting in which linear algebra happens. A vector space V is a set (the elements of which are called **vectors**) on which two operations are defined: vectors can be added together, and vectors can be multiplied by real numbers[1] called **scalars**. V must satisfy

(i)   There exists an additive identity (written **0**) in V such that $\mathbf{x} + \mathbf{0} = \mathbf{x}$ for all $\mathbf{x} \in V$

(ii) For every $\mathbf{x} \in V$, there exists an additive inverse (written $-\mathbf{x}$) such that $\mathbf{x} + (-\mathbf{x}) = \mathbf{0}$

(iii) There exists a multiplicative identity (written 1) in R such that $1\mathbf{x} = \mathbf{x}$ for all $\mathbf{x} \in V$

(iv) Commutativity: $\mathbf{x} + \mathbf{y} = \mathbf{y} + \mathbf{x}$ for all $\mathbf{x}, \mathbf{y} \in V$

(v) Associativity: $(\mathbf{x} + \mathbf{y}) + \mathbf{z} = \mathbf{x} + (\mathbf{y} + \mathbf{z})$ and $\alpha(\beta\mathbf{x}) = (\alpha\beta)\mathbf{x}$ for all $\mathbf{x}, \mathbf{y}, \mathbf{z} \in V$ and $\alpha, \beta \in$ R

---

[1] More generally, vector spaces can be defined over any **field** F. We take F = R in this document to avoid an unnecessary diversion into abstract algebra.

(vi) Distributivity: $\alpha(\mathbf{x} + \mathbf{y}) = \alpha\mathbf{x} + \alpha\mathbf{y}$ and $(\alpha + \beta)\mathbf{x} = \alpha\mathbf{x} + \beta\mathbf{x}$ for all $\mathbf{x}, \mathbf{y} \in V$ and $\alpha, \beta \in \mathrm{R}$

A set of vectors $\mathbf{v}_1, ..., \mathbf{v}_n \in V$ is said to be **linearly independent** if

$$\alpha_1\mathbf{v}_1 + \cdots + \alpha_n\mathbf{v}_n = \mathbf{0} \qquad \text{implies} \qquad \alpha_1 = \cdots = \alpha_n = 0.$$

The **span** of $\mathbf{v}_1, ..., \mathbf{v}_n \in V$ is the set of all vectors that can be expressed of a linear combination of them:

$$\text{span}\{\mathbf{v}_1, ..., \mathbf{v}_n\} = \{\mathbf{v} \in V : \exists \alpha_1, ..., \alpha_n$$
$$\text{such that } \alpha_1\mathbf{v}_1 + \cdots + \alpha_n\mathbf{v}_n = \mathbf{v}\}$$

If a set of vectors is linearly independent and its span is the whole of V, those vectors are said to be a **basis** for V. In fact, every linearly independent set of vectors forms a basis for its span.

If a vector space is crossed by a finite number of vectors, it is said to be **finite-dimensional**. Otherwise it is **infinite-dimensional**. The number of vectors in a basis for a finite-dimensional vector space V is called the **dimension** of V and denoted $\dim V$.

$$[2 \quad 5] \to \text{Row Vector}$$

$$\begin{bmatrix} 1 & -8 \\ 7 & 3 \end{bmatrix} \to \text{Matrix (No. of rows x No. of Columns)}$$

$$\begin{matrix} 1 & 0 & 0 \\ 0 & 1 & 0 \\ 0 & 0 & 1 \end{matrix}$$

2.2.3 Euclidean Space

Euclidean space is used to mathematically signify physical space, with notions such as distance, length, and angles. Although it becomes hard to visualize for $n > 3$, these ideas simplify mathematically in clear ways. Even when you're working in more general settings than R^n, it is often useful to visualize vector addition and scalar multiplication in terms of 2D vectors in the plane or 3D vectors in space.

2.2.4 Subspaces

Vector spaces can comprise other vector spaces. If V is a vector space, then $S \subseteq V$ is said to be a **subspace** of V if

(i) $\mathbf{0} \in S$

(ii) S is closed under addition: $\mathbf{x,y} \in S$ implies $\mathbf{x} + \mathbf{y} \in S$

(iii) S is closed under scalar multiplication: $\mathbf{x} \in S, \alpha \in \mathbb{R}$ implies $\alpha\mathbf{x} \in S$

Note that V is constantly a subspace of V, as is the trivial vector space which contains only $\mathbf{0}$.

As a concrete example, a line passing through the origin is a subspace of Euclidean space.

If U and W are subspaces of V, then their sum is defined as

$$U + W = \{\mathbf{u} + \mathbf{w} \mid \mathbf{u} \in U, \mathbf{w} \in W\}$$

2.2.5 Matrices

Matrices show a very important role in linear algebra. They will be used to efficiently signify systems of linear equations. Before we discuss some of these fascinating topics, allow us to initial outline what a matrix is and how much operations we can do with matrices.

A Matrix is an ordered 2D array of numbers and it has 2 indices. The initial one points to the row and the second to the column. For example, M23 refers to the value in the second row and therefore the third column, that is eight within the yellow graphic above. A Matrix can have multiple numbers of rows and columns. Note that a Vector is also a Matrix, however with solely one row or one column.

The Matrix in the example in the yellow graphic is also a 2- by 3-dimensional Matrix (rows x columns). Below you can see another example of a Matrix along with its notation:

$$\begin{bmatrix} u11 & \cdots & u1n \\ \vdots & \ddots & \vdots \\ um1 & \cdots & umn \end{bmatrix}$$

2.2.6 Vector

A vector is an array of numbers. The numbers are organized so as. We tend to can identify every individual variety by its index in that ordering. Typically, we have a tendency to provide vectors lower case names written in daring kind face, like x. The elements of the vector are identified by writing its name in italic kind face, with a subscript.

For example, V2 refers to the second value within the Vector, which is -8 in the graphic above

$$\begin{bmatrix} x1 \\ \vdots \\ xn \end{bmatrix}$$

2.2.7 Tensors

You can imagine of a Tensor as an array of numbers, settled on a daily grid, with a variable variety of machetes. A Tensor has 3 directories, where the first points to the row, the 2nd to the column and the 3rd one to the axis. For example,

T232 points to the 2nd row, the third column, and the second axis

3	1	4	1
5	9	2	6
4	7	6	3
1	4	8	9
7	2	3	2
7	2	3	0

tensor of dimensions [6,4]

Tensor is the most universal term for all of these concepts above because a Tensor is a multi-dimensional array and it can be a Vector and a Matrix, depending on the number of directories it has. For example, a 1st order Tensor would be a Vector (1 index). A 2nd Tensor is a Matrix (2 indices) and 3rd order Tensors (3 indices) and higher are called Higher-Order Tensors (3 or more indices).

2.2.8 Computational Rules

2.2.8.1 Matrix Scalar Operations

Multiplying a Matrix by a Vector will be theoretical of as multiplying individually row of the Matrix by the column of the Vector. The output will be a Vector that has the same variety of rows because the Matrix.

2.2.8.2 Matrix-Matrix Addition & Subtraction

Matrix-Matrix Addition and Subtraction is honestly simple and straight-forward. The condition is that the matrices have the like dimensions and the result is a Matrix that has additionally the like dimensions. You only add or subtract separately price of the primary Matrix with its matching value in the second Matrix.

2.2.8.3 Matrix Multiplication

Multiplying 2 Matrices collected isn't that hard either if you know the way to multiply a Matrix by a Vector. You will solely multiply Matrices along if the number of the 1st Matrix's columns matches the number of the second Matrix's rows. The result will be a Matrix with the identical range of rows as the primary Matrix and the identical number of columns as the 2nd Matrix. It works as follows:

You just divided the second Matrix into column-Vectors and multiply the first Matrix separately by each of those Vectors. Then you place the results in a new Matrix.

2.2.8.3.1 Matrix Multiplication Properties

Matrix Multiplication has numerous belongings that allow us to bundle a lot of computation into one Matrix multiplication. We will discuss them one by one below. We will start by explaining these concepts with Scalars and then with Matrices because this will give you a better recognizing of the process.

1. Not Commutative

Scalar Multiplication is commutative but Matrix Multiplication is not. This means that when we are multiplying Scalars, 6×3 is the same as 3×6. But when we multiply Matrices by every other, A×B isn't the same as B×A.

A×B≠B×A   (in Matrices)

2. Associative

Scalar and Matrix Multiplication are together associative. This means that the Scalar multiplication 2(5×2) is the same as (2×5)2 and that the Matrix multiplication A(B×C) is the same as (A×B) C.

$$A(B×C) = (A×B)\ C$$

3. Distributive

Scalar and Matrix Multiplication are too both distributive. This means that 2(5 + 2) is the same as 2×5 + 2×2 and that A(B+C) is the same as A×B + A×C.

$$A(B+C) = A×B + A×C$$

4. Identity Matrix

The Identity Matrix is a distinct kind of Matrix but first, we necessity to define what an Identity is. The number one is an Identity because all you multiply with one is equal to itself. Therefore, every Matrix that is multiplied by an Identity Matrix is equal to itself. For example, Matrix A times its Identity-Matrix is equal to A.

You can do an Identity Matrix by

the fact that it has ones along its diagonals and that every other value is zero. It is also a "squared matrix," meaning that its number of rows matches its number of columns. We formerly discussed that Matrix multiplication is not commutative (A×B≠B×A) but there is one exemption, namely if we multiply a Matrix by an Identity Matrix. Therefore, the following equation is true: A×I = I×A = A

2.2.8.4 Inverse and Transpose

The Matrix-Transpose and the Matrix-Inverse are two dislike kinds of Matrix properties. Again, we will start by debating how these properties relate to real numbers and then how they relate to Matrices.

2.2.9 Summary

In this section, you learned about the mathematical objects of Linear Algebra that are utilized in Machine Learning. You learned how to multiply, divide, add and subtract these mathematical objects. Moreover, you've got learned regarding the foremost important properties of Matrices and why they empower us to make additional economical computations.

On top of that, you have cleared your ideas what inverse and transpose Matrices are and what you'll be able to do with them. Although there are also other elements of Linear Algebra employed in Machine Learning, this post gave you a proper introduction to the most necessary concepts.

2.3 Multivariate Calculus

Recognizing calculus is central to recognizing machine learning! You'll be able to imagine of calculus as simply a group of tools for analyzing the connection between functions and their inputs. Typically, in machine learning, we tend to are attempting to find the inputs which permit a perform to best match the information.

We tend to start this module from the basics, by recalling what a perform is and where we have a tendency to would possibly encounter one. Following this, we tend to talk concerning the how, when sketching a perform on a graph, the slope describes the speed of modification off the output with respect to an input. Using this visual intuition, we next derive a robust mathematical definition of a by-product, that we tend to then use to dislike some interesting functions.

Making on the foundations of the previous module, we have a tendency to currently generalize our calculus tools to handle multivariable systems. This means that we can take a perform with multiple inputs and verify the influence of each of them separately. It would not be

48

unusual for a machine learning process to need the analysis of a operate with thousands of inputs, so we can conjointly introduce the linear algebra structures necessary for storing the results of our multivariate calculus analysis in an orderly fashion.

2.3.1 Derivative

A derivative can be defined in two ways:

- Instantaneous rate of change (Physics)
- Slope of a line at a precise point (Geometry)

Both show the same principle, but for our purposes it's easier to explain using the geometric definition.

$$\text{Slope} = \frac{Change\ in\ y}{Change\ in\ x}$$

A derivative output an expression we can use to calculate the instantaneous rate of change, or slope, at a single point on a line. After solving for the derivative, you can use it to calculate the slope at every other point on the line.

- Step by Step

Calculating the derivative is the same as calculating normal slope, however in this case we calculate the slope between our point and a point infinitesimally close to it. We use the variable h to show this infinitesimally distance. Here are the steps:

1. Given the function:

$$f(x)=x^2$$

2. Increment x by a very small value $h(h=\Delta x)$

$$f(x+h)=(x+h)^2$$

3. Apply the slope formula

$$\frac{f(x+h)-f(x)}{h}$$

4. Simplify the equation

$$\frac{x^2+2xh+h^2-x^2}{h}$$

$$\frac{2xh+h^2}{h}=2x+h$$

5. Set h to 0 (the limit as h heads toward 0)

$$2x+0=2x$$

So, what does this mean? It means for the function f(x)=x2f(x)=x2, the slope at any point equals 2x2x. The formula is defined as:

$$\lim_{h \to 0} \frac{f(x+h) - f(x)}{h}$$

2.3.2 Machine Learning use Cases

Machine learning uses derivatives in optimization problems. Optimization algorithms like gradient descent use derivatives to decide whether to increase or decrease weights in order to maximize or minimize some objective (e.g. a model's accuracy or error functions). Derivatives also assist us approximate nonlinear functions as linear functions (tangent lines), which have constant slopes. With a constant slope we can decide whether to move up or down the slope (increase or decrease our weights) to get closer to the target value (class label).

2.3.3 Chain Rule

The chain rule is a formula for calculating the derivatives of composite functions. Composite functions are functions composed of functions inside other function(s).

Given a composite function f(x)=A(B(x)), the derivative of f(x) equals the product of the derivative of A with respect to B(x) and the derivative of B with respect to x.

composite function derivative=outer function derivative × inner function derivative

For example,

f(x)=h(g(x))

The chain rule tells us the derivative of f(x) equals to

$$\frac{dy}{dx} = \frac{dh}{dg} \times \frac{dg}{dx}$$

2.3.4 Gradient

A gradient could be a vector that saves the partial derivatives of multivariable functions. It assists us calculate the slope at a precise point on a curve for functions with multiple freelance variables. In order to calculate this a lot of tough slope, we tend to require to isolate every variable to work out how it impacts the output on its own.

To do that we have a tendency to iterate through each of the variables and calculate the spinoff of the function after holding all different variables constant. Each iteration produces a partial spinoff that we tend to save in the gradient.

2.3.5 Partial Derivative

In functions with 2 or more variables, the partial derivative is the derivative of one variable with respect to the others. If we change x, but hold all other variables constant, how does $f(x, z)$ change? That's one partial derivative. The next variable is z. If we change z but hold xx constant, how does $f(x, z)$ change? We save partial derivatives in a gradient, which shows the full derivative of the multivariable function.

2.4 Probability Theory

Why do we require probabilities when we already have such a great mathematical tooling? We have calculus to work with functions on the infinitesimal scale and to measure how they change. We developed algebra to solve equations, and we have dozens of other areas of mathematics that assist us to tackle almost any kind of hard problem we can imagine of.

The difficult part is that we all live in a chaotic universe where things can't be measured exactly most of the time. When we study real world processes, we want to learn about numerous random events that distort our experiments. Uncertainty is everywhere and we must take it to be used for our requires. That is when probability theory and statistics come into play.

We will go through various views on probability theory below.

2.4.1 Frequentist Probabilities

Imagine we were given a coin and want to check whether it is fair or not. How do we approach this? Let's try to conduct some experiments and record 1 if heads come up and 0 if we see tails. Repeat this 1000 tosses and count every 0 and 1. After we had some tedious time experimenting, we got those results: 600 heads (1s) and 400 tails (0s).

If we then count how frequent heads or tails came up in the past, we will get 60% and 40% respectively. Those frequencies can be interpreted as probabilities of a coin coming up heads or tails. This is called a frequentist view on the probabilities.

2.4.2 Conditional Probabilities

Frequently we want to know the probability of an event given some other event has occurred. We write conditional probability of an event A given event B as P (A | B).

2.4.3 Dependent and Independent Events

Events are called independent if the probability of one event does not influence the other in any way. Take for example the probability of rolling a dice and getting a 2 for the first time and for the second time. Those events are independent. We can state this as

$$P(\text{roll2}) = P(\text{roll2}_{\text{1st time}})P(\text{roll2}_{\text{2nd time}})$$

But why this formula works? First, let's rename events for 1st and 2nd tosses as A and B to remove notational clutter and then rewrite probability of a roll explicitly as joint probability of both rolls we had seen so far:

$$P(A,B) = P(A)P(B)$$

And now multiply and divide P(A) by P(B) (nothing changes, it can be cancelled out) and recall the definition of conditional probability:

$$P(A) = \frac{P(A)P(B)}{P(B)} = \frac{P(A,B)}{P(B)} = P(A|B)$$

If we read expression above from right to left we find that P(A | B) = P(A). Basically, this means that A is independent of B! The same argument goes for P(B) and we are done.

2.4.4 Distributions

What is a probability distribution anyways? It is a law that tells us probabilities of dislike possible outcomes in some experiment formulated as a mathematical function. As every function, a distribution may have some parameters to adjust its behavior.

When we measured relative frequencies of a coin toss event, we have actually calculated a so-called empirical probability distribution. It turns out that many uncertain processes in our world can be formulated in terms of probability distributions. For example, our coin outcomes have a Bernoulli distribution and if we wanted to calculate a probability of heads after n trials, we may use a Binomial distribution.

It is convenient to introduce a concept analogous

to a variable that may be used in probabilistic environments — a random variable. Every random variable has some distribution assigned to it. Radom variables are written in upper case by convention, and we may use ~ symbol to specify a distribution assigned to a variable.

2.4.5 Basic Rules & Models

Probability gives the information about how likely an event can occur. Digging into the terminology of the probability:

Trial or Experiment: The act that leads to a result with certain possibility.
Sample space: The set of all possible outcomes of an experiment.
Event: Non-empty subset of sample space is known as event.

So, in technical terms, probability is the measure of how likely an event is when an experiment is conducted.

Chapter 3: Fundamentals of Deep Learning

3.1 Introduction

Deep structured learning or classified learning or deep learning in brief is part of the family of machine learning approaches which are themselves a subset of the broad field of Artificial Intelligence.

Deep learning is a class of machine learning algorithms that use some layers of nonlinear processing units for features mining and transformation. Every succeeding layer uses the output from the previous layer as input.

Deep neural networks, deep belief networks and recurrent neural networks have been applied to arenas such as speech recognition, computer vision, natural language processing, machine translation, audio recognition, social network filtering and bioinformatics where they delivered results like to and, in some cases, better than human experts have.

Deep Learning Algorithms and Networks –

- are based on the unsupervised learning of multiple levels of features or depictions of the data. Higher-level features are resultant from lower level features to form a hierarchical illustration.

- use some form of gradient descent for training.

Deep Learning is a subfield of machine learning concerned with algorithms inspired by the structure and function of the brain called artificial neural networks.

If you are just starting out in the field of deep learning or you had some experience with neural networks some time ago, you may be confused. I know I was confused initially and so were many of my colleagues and friends who learned and used neural networks in the 1990s and early 2000s.

The leaders and experts in the field have ideas of what deep learning is and these precise and nuanced perspectives shed a lot of light on what deep learning is all about.

Deep Learning could be categorized into three major classes based on the purposes they are designed for:

Unsupervised or generative learning deep networks aim to capture high-order correlation of unlabeled input data for pattern recognition or synthesis purposes. When being used to classify joint statistical distributions of the experimental data and their related classes, the networks feature reproductive mode and could be altered into discriminative ones for more learning.

Supervised learning networks are used when target label data are available, where the models could directly deliver discriminative power for classification purposes.

Hybrid deep networks are the combinations of two kinds of networks mentioned above so that unsupervised deep networks could deliver excellent initialization based on which discrimination could be examined. We will introduce some precise networks under every type and deliver their corresponding applications in the primary of finance.

3.2 Terms & Concepts

Following terminologies and notions are part and parcel of deep learning.

To support you identify many terminologies, The terms are categorized in three dislike groups.

- Basics of Neural Networks
- Convolutional Neural Networks
- Recurrent Neural Networks

3.2.1 Basics of Neural Networks

- Neuron:

  It's sort of a neuron procedure the straightforward part of our brain, a neuron procedure the elementary structure of a neural network. Just imagine of what we have a tendency to do once we get new data. After we get the info, we process it and then we have a tendency to manufacture an output. Likewise, in case of a neural network, a neuron accepts an input, processes it and produces an output that is additionally sent to alternative neurons for more processing or it is the last output.

- Weights:
  When input arrives the neuron, it's multiplied by a weight. For sample, if a neuron has 2 inputs, then every input will have a connected weight allotted to it. We tend to initialize the weights arbitrarily and these weights are rationalized throughout the model training process. The neural network after training assigns a better weight to the input it ponders a lot of important as connected to the ones which are measured less necessary. A weight of zero suggests that that the actual feature is unimportant.

- Bias:
- In addition to the weights, another linear module is implemented to the input, known as the bias. It is added to

the result of weight multiplication to the input. The bias is fundamentally added to modification the range of the load multiplied input. After adding the bias, the result would seem like a×W1+bias. This is that the last linear module of the input alteration.

- Activation Function:

  Once the linear part is implemented to the input, a non-linear operate is applied to it. This is done by applying the activation function to the linear combination. The activation perform interprets the input signals to output signals. The output when application of the activation perform would look one thing like f(a×W1+b) where f() is that the activation function.

3.2.2 Convolutional Neural Networks

- Filters:

  A filter in a CNN is like a weight matrix with which we multiply a part of the input image to generate a convoluted output. Consider we have an image of size 28×28. We arbitrarily allocate a filter of size 3×3, which is then multiplied with dislike 3×3 sections of the image to form what is known as a convoluted output. The filter size is usually smaller than the original image size. The filter values are upgraded like weight values during back-propagation for cost minimization.

- Pooling:

  It is usually to periodically introduce pooling layers in between the convolution layers. This is essentially done to reduce a number of parameters and stop over-fitting. The most common kind of pooling is a pooling layer of filter size (2,2) using the MAX operation.

- Padding:

  Padding mentions to adding extra layer of zeros diagonally the images so that the output image has the same size as the input. This is known as like padding.

- Data Augmentation:

  Knowledge Augmentation mentions to the addition of recent information resulting from the assumed data, which may influence be useful for guess. For example, it might be easier to view the cat during a dark image if you brighten it, or as an example, a nine within the digit recognition might be slightly tilted or rotated. In this case, rotation would resolve the problem and increase the accuracy of our model. By rotating or brightening we're refining the quality of our knowledge. This is called Information augmentation.

3.2.3 Recurrent Neural Network

- Recurrent Neuron:

  A recurrent neuron is single in which the output of the neuron is referred back to it for t time stamps. If your facet at the diagram the output is distributed back as input 't' times. The unrolled neuron appearances like 't' dislike neurons connected with each alternative. The basic advantage of this neuron is that it gives a broader spread output.

- RNN:

  Recurrent neural networks are used particularly for sequential knowledge where the sooner output is employed to guess the next one. In this circumstance the networks have loops within them. The loops inside the hidden neuron provides them the potential to avoid wasting data about the previous words for a while to be in a position to guess the output. The output of the hidden layer is referred once more to the hidden layer for 't' time stamps. The un-folded neuron appearance like the above diagram. The output of the recurrent neuron goes to the next layer only when implementation incessantly stamps. The output sent is more generalized and the preceding info is retained for a lengthier period.

- Vanishing Gradient Problem:

  Vanishing gradient drawback arises in cases where the gradient of the activation operate is very small. During back propagation when the weights are multiplied with these small gradients, they incline to develop very tiny and "vanish" as they are going deeper within the network. This makes the neural network to forget the long-vary dependency. This usually converts a problem in cases of recurring neural networks where long-term dependences are very vital for the network to evoke.

3.3 How Deep Learning Works

Computer programs that use deep learning reconsider a lot of the like method. Individually algorithm in the grading applies a nonlinear alteration on its input and uses what it learns to create a statistical model as output. Repetitions endure until the output has grasped a suitable level of accuracy. The variety of dispensation layers through that information must pass is what impressed the label deep.

Deep learning gets its name from how it's used to look at "unstructured" information, or information that hasn't been before labeled by additional source and might essential definition. That needs careful analysis of what the information is, and repeated tests of that information to end up with a final, practical conclusion. Computers aren't conventionally smart at examining unstructured data like this.

Imagine about it in terms of writing: If you had ten folks transcribe the identical word, that word would look very dislike from every person, from sloppy to neat, and from cursive to print. The human brain has no drawback recognizing that it's all the identical word, as a result of it knows how words, writing, paper, ink, and personal quirks all work. A traditional laptop system, however, would have no means of important that those words are the same, because all of them look therefore dislike.

Use cases today for deep learning contain all types of huge information analytics applications, especially those targeted on natural language processing (NLP), language translation, medical diagnosis, stock market trading signals, network security and image identification.

3.3.1 Deep Learning Architecture

Generative deep architectures, which are intended to characterize the high-order correlation properties of the observed or visible data for pattern analysis or synthesis purposes, and/or characterize the joint statistical distributions of the visible data and their related classes. In the latter case, the use of Bayes rule can turn this kind of architecture into a discriminative one.

Discriminative deep architectures, which are intended to directly offer discriminative power for pattern classification, often by characterizing the posterior distributions of classes conditioned on the visible data.

Hybrid deep architectures, where the goal is discrimination but is assisted (often in a significant way) with the outcomes of generative architectures via better optimization or/and regularization, or discriminative criteria are used to learn the parameters in any of the deep generative models.

3.4 Using Neural Networks

A kind of innovative machine learning algorithm, identified as neural networks, underpins most deep learning models. Neural networks come back in several dislike forms, together with recurrent neural networks, convolutional neural networks, artificial neural networks and feedforward neural networks, and every has their advantage for precise use cases. However, they all perform in somewhat like ways in which, by feeding information in and letting the model figure out for itself whether it's created the correct interpretation or choice concerning a given information component.

Neural networks involve a trial-and-error process; thus, they need huge amounts of data to train on. It's no coincidence that neural networks became common solely after most enterprises embraced massive knowledge analytics and picked up huge saves of data. Because the model's 1st few repetitions involve somewhat-educated guesses on the contents of image or elements of speech, the information used during the training stage must be labeled therefore the model will see if its guess was accurate.

This means that, though several initiatives that use huge data have large amounts of knowledge, unstructured information is a smaller amount cooperative. Unstructured data can be analyzed by a deep learning model once it's been trained and reveries an appropriate level of accuracy, however deep learning models can't train on unstructured knowledge.

3.5 Applications

Because deep learning models process information in ways like to the human brain, models can be applied to many tasks people do. Deep learning is currently used in most common image recognition tools, NLP processing and speech recognition software. These tools are starting to appear in applications as diverse as self-driving cars and language translation services.

3.5.1 Image Recognition

Image recognition, in the context of machine vision, is the aptitude of software to spot objects, places, people, writing and actions in images. Computers can use machine vision technologies together with a camera and artificial intelligence software to attain image recognition.

Image recognition is employed to do a giant variety of machine-primarily based visual tasks, such as labeling the content of images with meta-tags, doing image content search and guiding autonomous robots, self-driving cars and accident avoidance systems.

While human and animal brains determine objects with

ease, computers have issue with the task. Software for image recognition needs deep machine learning. Performance is best on convolutional neural net processors as the precise task otherwise wants huge amounts of power for its compute-intensive nature.

Image recognition algorithms will perform by use of comparative 3D models, entrances from dislike angles using edge detection or by elements. Image recognition algorithms are usually trained on many pre-labeled photos with guided laptop learning.

Privacy concerns over image recognition and like technologies are provocative as these corporations will pull a huge volume of data from user photos uploaded to their social media websites like Facebook, twitter etc.

3.5.2 Facial Recognition

Facial recognition could be a type of biometric software that maps an individual's facial options mathematically and saves the information as a faceprint. The software uses deep learning algorithms to associate a live detention or digital image to the saved faceprint in command to confirm an individual's identity. High-quality cameras in mobile devices have finished facial recognition a possible possibility for authentication as well as ID. Apple's iPhone X, for instance, contains Face ID technology that lets users unlock their phones with a faceprint mapped by the phone's camera.

The phone's software, that is meant with 3-D modeling to fight being deceived by photos or masks, captures and equates over 30,00zero variables. As of this writing, Face ID will be used to authenticate purchases with Apple Pay and, in the iTunes, Save, App Save and iBooks Save. Apple encodes and saves faceprint data within the cloud, however authentication takes place directly on the device.

Developers will use Amazon Recognition, an image analysis service that's half of the Amazon AI suite, to feature facial recognition and analysis features to an application. The technology, which uses machine learning to note, match and classify faces, is being employed in a broad variety of ways that, together with entertainment and marketing.

While a private is tagged in a very photograph, the software saves mapping info concerning that person's facial properties. Once sufficient information has been composed, the software can use that info to spot an explicit person's face when it looks in an exceedingly new photograph. To protect individuals' privacy, a feature known as Photo Review notifies the Facebook member who has been identified.

Currently, there are no laws in the United States that exactly defend someone's biometric data. Facial recognition systems are currently being studied or installed for airport security and it's estimated that additional than [*fr1] the United States population has currently had their faceprint taken.

According the Department of Homeland Security, the only approach to avoid having biometric information collected when traveling internationally is to avoid from traveling. The General Information Protection Regulation (GDPR) for European Member States does speech biometric knowledge.

3.5.3 Speech Recognition

In speech processing, speech waveform is usually split to short segments (5–30msec) and assumed that the speech signal is stationary within these short frames. This is called the quasi-stationary property of speech waveforms.

Standard deep learning process operate on this domain to classify every frame to a certain speech unit (depends on the language, typically phoneme for English).

Talking more voice interface Speech recognition technology has become an increasingly popular concept in recent years. From organizations to individuals, the technology is broadly used for various advantages it delivers.

One of the most notable advantages of speech recognition technology contains the dictation capability it delivers. With the assist of the technology users can easily control devices and create documents by speaking. Speech recognition can allow documents to be created faster because the software generally produces words as fast as they are spoken, which is generally much faster than a person can kind.

No one will be spelling or writing hold you back. Voice recognition software, as being faster to finish tasks, is gradually accurate when it comes to vocabulary and spelling.

For most of us, the ultimate luxury would be an assistant who always listens for your call, anticipates your every need, and takes action when necessary. That luxury is now available thanks to artificial intelligence assistants, as known as voice assistants.

Voice assistants are available in somewhat small packages and can do a different of actions after hearing a wake word or command. They can answer questions, play music, turn on lights, place online orders, etc.

But, for independent makers and entrepreneurs, it's hard to make a simple speech detector using open source code. Many voice recognition datasets require preprocessing before a neural network model can be built on them. To assist with this, TensorFlow had unconfined the Speech Commands Datasets. It holds 65,000 one-second long words of 30 short words, by thousands of dislike people.

3.6 Future of Deep Learning

The way forward for deep learning is largely bright! The best issue about a neural network is that it proceeds at trade with a vast amount of dissimilar knowledge. That's particularly relevant in our era of advanced good sensors, which can gather a fantastic quantity of knowledge. Old-vogue computer solutions are beginning to fight with sorting, labeling and drawing deductions from thus a lot of knowledge and data.

Chapter 4: Natural Language Processing

4.1 Introduction

Deep learning process are achieving state-of-the-art results on challenging machine learning problems such as describing photos and translating text from one language to another.

Natural language processing (NLP) deals with making computational algorithms to automatically analyze and show human language. NLP-based systems have empowered a broad range of applications such as Google's powerful search engine, and more newly, Amazon's voice assistant named Alexa. NLP is also useful to every machine the capability to do difficult natural language related chaos such as machine translation and dialogue generation.

Natural Language Processing (NLP) is a sub-field of Artificial Intelligence that is fixated on empowering computers to recognize and procedure human languages, to become computers closer to a human-level considerate of language. Computers don't yet have the same instinctive recognizing of natural language that humans do. They can't really recognize what the language is really trying to say. In a nutshell, a computer can't read between the lines.

NLP is a way for computers to analyze, recognize, and derive meaning from human language in a smart and useful way. By utilizing NLP, developers can organize and structure knowledge to do tasks such as automatic summarization, named entity recognition translation, relationship mining, speech recognition, sentiment analysis, and topic segmentation.

That being said, recent advances in Machine Learning (ML) have empowered computers to do pretty a lot of useful things with natural language! Deep Learning has empowered us to write programs to do things like language translation, semantic recognizing, and text summarization. All of them are added real-world value, making it easy for you to distinguish and do computations on large blocks of text without the manual effort.

The development of NLP has its meaning because of some precise problems and phenomena that arrive when we study natural language. Most of the times, these problems are unique in comparison to the problems that emerge in other arenas of computer science or engineering, and that is in part what makes NLP such an interesting and dislike area.

Natural Language Processing (NLP) refers to AI process of communicating with intelligent systems using a natural language such as English.

Processing of Natural Language is required when you want an intelligent system like robot to do as per your instructions, when you want to catch choice from a dialogue based clinical expert system, etc.

The field of NLP includes making computers reform useful tasks with the natural language's humans use. The input and output of an NLP system can be –

- Speech
- Written Text

4.2 Components of NLP

In this section, we will learn about the dislike components of NLP. There are two components of NLP. The components are described below −

Natural Language Recognizing (NLU)

It includes the following tasks −

- Charting the given input in natural language into useful show.
- Evaluating dislike aspects of the language.

Natural Language Generation (NLG)

It is the process of producing meaningful phrases and sentences in the form of natural language from some internal show. It includes −

- Text planning − This cover regaining the relevant material from the knowledge base.
- Sentence planning − This contains choosing the required words, forming meaningful phrases, setting tone of the sentence.
- Text Realization − This is mapping sentence plan into sentence structure.

4.3 NLP Terminologies

Let us now see a few important terms in the NLP terminology.

Phonology – It is study of forming sound methodically.

Morphology – It is a learning of building of words from primeval expressive units.

Morpheme – It is a embryonic unit of sense in a language.

Syntax – It denotes to positioning words to make a sentence. It also includes determining the structural role of words in the sentence and in phrases.

Semantics – It is concerned with the meaning of words and how to combine words into meaningful phrases and sentences.

Pragmatics – It deals with using and recognizing sentences in dislike situations and how the understanding of the sentence is pretentious.

Discourse – It deals with how the directly preceding sentence can affect the understanding of the next sentence.

World Knowledge – It contains the over-all information about the world

4.4 Steps in NLP

There are general five steps:

- **Lexical Analysis**:

  It includes classifying and evaluating the construction of words. Lexicon of a language means the group of words and phrases in a language. Lexical investigation is dividing the whole chunk of txt into paragraphs, words, and sentences.

- **Syntactic Analysis (Parsing)**:

  It includes analysis of words in the sentence for grammar and arranging words in a manner that shows the relationship among the words. The sentence such as "The school goes to boy" is rejected by English syntactic analyzer.

- **Semantic Analysis:**

  It draws the exact meaning or the dictionary meaning from the text. The text is checked for significance. It is done by mapping syntactic structures and objects in the task domain. The semantic analyzer disrespects sentence such as "hot ice-cream".

- **Discourse Integration:**

The meaning of any sentence depends upon the meaning of the sentence just before it. It also carries about the meaning of immediately succeeding sentence.

- **Pragmatic Analysis:**

During this, what was said is re-interpreted on what it actually meant. It includes deriving those aspects of language which require real world knowledge.

4.5 Applications of Deep Learning for NLP

The arena of natural language processing is ever-changing from statistical process to neural network process.

There are still many fascinating issues to resolve in natural language. Nonetheless, deep learning process are achieving state-of-the-art results on some precise language problems.

Deep learning models on normal problems that's most attention-grabbing; it's the detail that a sole model can learn word meaning and do language tasks, removing the require for a pipeline of specific and hand-crafted method.

In this section, we will look at the following 7 natural language processing problems.

- Text Classification:
- Machine Translation
- Document Summarization
- Language Modeling
- Speech Recognition
- Caption Generation
- Question Answering

Chapter 5: Artificial Neural Networks &

Deep Neural Networks

5.1 Artificial Neural Networks

Neural networks are an entire set of algorithms, modeled insecurely once the human brain, that are supposed to categorize patterns. They understand sensual data through a quite machine perception, labeling or clustering raw input. The patterns they determine are numerical, confined in vectors, into that all real-world information, be it images, sound, text or time series, must be decoded.

Neural networks assist us cluster and classify. You'll imagine of them as a clustering and classification layer on prime of the information you save and organize. They assist to cluster unlabeled data consistent with liceities among the instance inputs, and that they classify information when they have a labeled dataset to train on. (Neural networks can additionally derive the options that are nourished to alternative algorithms for clustering and classification; so, you can imagine of deep neural networks as elements of larger machine-learning applications as well as algorithms for reinforcement learning, regression and classification)

5.1.1 Neural Networks Elements

Deep learning is the name we have a tendency to use for "stacked neural networks"; that's, networks collected of the many layers.

The layers are made of nodes. A node is just a place where calculation occurs, loosely patterned on a neuron within the human brain, that fires when it conferences enough stimuli. A node syndicates input from the information with a set of numbers, or weights, that either amplify or dampen that input, thereby assigning significance to inputs for the task the algorithm is tiresome to learn. These input-weight merchandises are added and the results of summation is ignored a node's so-called activation perform, to seek out whether or not and to what extent that signal progresses a lot of through the network to disturb the eventual outcome, say, an act of classification.

5.1.2 How Artificial Neural Networks Work

A neural network usually includes a giant variety of processors operating in parallel and arranged in tiers. The first tier accepts the raw input information --

analogous to optic nerves in human visual processing. Every successive tier accepts the output from the tier previous it, slightly than from the raw input -- in the similar method neurons additional from the optic nerve settle for signals from those nearer to it. The last tier produces the output of the system.

Every processing node has its own minor sphere of knowledge, as well as what it's seen and any rules it absolutely was initially programmed with or developed for itself. The tiers are highly interconnected, that means every node in tier n will be linked to several nodes in tier n-one-- its inputs -- and in tier none, which brings input for those nodes. There may be one or multiple nodes in the output layer, from that the solution it produces can be read.

Neural networks are notable for being adaptive, which suggests that they alter themselves as they learn from initial training and following runs deliver additional info regarding the world. The most basic learning model is focused on weighting the input streams, that is how each node weights the importance of input from every of its precursors. Inputs that contribute to getting right answers are weighted advanced.

5.1.3 How Neural Networks Learn

Typically, a neural network is initially trained or nourished big amounts of knowledge. Coaching contains of providing input and telling the network what the output should be. For example, to make a network to detect the faces of actors, initial training may be a series of photos of actors, non-actors, masks, statuary, animal faces and so on.

Every input is attended by the matching ID, like actors' names, "not actor" or "not human" info. Providing the responses permits the model to regulate its internal weightings to amass how to do its work improved.

In important the principles and creating determinations -- that's, every node chooses what to send on to a higher tier primarily based on its own inputs from the previous tier -- neural networks use many principles. These contain gradient-based mostly coaching, fuzzy logic, genetic algorithms and Bayesian method. They may be given some elementary instructions concerning object relationships within the house being modeled. For example, a facial recognition system might be instructed, "Eyebrows are found higher than eyes," or, "Moustaches are below a nose.

Moustaches are higher than and/or beside a mouth." Preloading rules will make exercise faster and make the model additional influential sooner. But it conjointly makes in assumptions regarding the nature of the problematic area, that could prove to be either irrelevant and unfaithful or incorrect and counterproductive, making the high-quality concerning what, if any, rules to create in very necessary.

5.2 Deep Neural Networks

Deep neural network (DNN) is an ANN with multiple hidden layers between the input and output layers. Like too shallow ANNs, DNNs will model multifaceted non-linear relationships.

The primary purpose of a neural network is to accept a set of inputs, do progressively troublesome calculations on them, and provide output to resolve planet problems like classification. We have a tendency to limit ourselves to feed forward neural networks.

Deep-learning networks are different from the a lot of ordinary single-hidden-layer neural networks by their penetration; that is, the amount of node layers through that information passes in a multistep process of pattern recognition.

Earlier versions of neural networks like the primary perceptrons were shallow, collected of 1 input and one output layer, and at most one hidden layer in between. More than three layers qualifies as "deep" learning. Thus deep could be a firmly clear, technical term which means more than one hidden layer.

In deep-learning networks, every layer of nodes trains on a separate set of options primarily based on the preceding layer's output. The more you advance into the neural internet, the additional tough the features your nodes can determine, since they calculate and re-mix features from the preceding layer.

Deep-learning networks do automatic feature mining without human interference, in contrast to most previous-style machine-learning algorithms. Given that feature mining may be a task which will take groups of data scientists years to realize, deep learning may be a manner to avoid the choke-point of limited specialists. It enlarges the powers of tiny information science teams, which by their nature don't scale.

When coaching on unlabeled data, every node layer in an exceedingly deep network learns options automatically by repeatedly trying to reconstruct the input from that it attracts its samples, trying to diminish the difference between the network's guesses and therefore the likelihood distribution of the input data itself. Limited Boltzmann machines, for examples, produce therefore-called reconstructions during this manner.

Chapter 6: Conclusion

6.1 Conclusion

In the initial days of AI, the sector quickly undertaken and solved difficulties that are intellectually arduous for human beings however comparatively straight-forward for computers-issues that may be labelled by a list of formal, mathematical rules. The true test to AI showed to be solving the tasks that are straightforward for folks to try and do but exhausting for individuals to designate formally-issues that we tend to solve instinctively, that feel involuntary, like knowing spoken words or faces in pictures.

This book can be useful for a selection of readers, students, Laptop Science graduates, however we wrote it with two primary goal audiences in mind. One of those goal audiences is university students (undergraduate or graduate) learning regarding Deep Learning, together with those who are beginning a career in deep learning and artificial intelligence analysis. The alternative goal audience is software engineers who do not have a deep learning or statistics background, but need to quickly get one and begin using deep learning in their product or platform. Deep learning has already established useful in several software disciplines along with robotics, chemistry, NLP computer vision, speech and audio processing, bio-informatics, video games, search engines, online advertising and finance.

We have a tendency to hope you have got enjoyed learning regarding "Deep Learning: A Comprehensive Guide for Beginners". Deep learning is a continuously developing field. Because of this, there are some issues to stay in mind as you're employed with Deep learning processes or analyze the impact of deep learning processes. Deep learning is an uninterruptedly emerging field. Because of this, there are some contemplations to stay in mind as you're employed with deep learning processes, or evaluate the impact of deep learning processes.

As you finished the book, I wish you the best of luck and encourage you to enjoy yourself as you go, tackling the content prepared for you and applying what you've learned to new areas or data.

Good Luck!